Emotions Stage

Shadow Series Volume One

Poetry
by
Faye Fleming

Note From The Author:
Poetry is one of the loveliest ways known to express ones self. Many words written in poetry can normally be translated several different ways, depending upon its reader. It can mean one thing to one person, and yet another to someone else. However, to me, the mystery is to ponder what the author had in mind during its creation. I have fully enjoyed the feed-back I have gotten from some of my readers on this set of poems. I dedicate Emotions Stage, to all that took part in my life, for planting the seeds of this work. Most of you know who you are & the garden in which you planted. Thank You, Faye

Faye Books Trademark

Publisher: Faye Books
Copyright © 2007 Faye Fleming
All rights reserved.
ISBN 978-0-6151-6371-0
Library of Congress Control Number: 2007937649
Printed in the United States of America

Emotions Stage can be ordered at: http://www.lulu.com

Email: fayefleming@hotmail.co.uk
Write: Faye Fleming (Writers Division)
P.O. Box 387 Shepherdsville, KY 40165

September 2007

First Edition

In the realm of in between ...
lies the things that go unseen.
Somewhere between daylight and dark...
Imagination begins to embark.
Cast a spell to weave a tale...then
lead them on a journey!

Table of Content

My Mind Is Whirling

I find no peace, I ask myself why?
As if an unknown power should answer.

Not knowing where I'm going,
remembering, only fragments of where I've been.

Everything an obsession...not normal at all.
I look around anxiously, hoping no one will notice –
Should I fall.

Why I should care?
I've not a clue! However, it's obvious, that I do!

The Wish

Running water…gentle waves…

Into shadowy dreaming,

she is saved.

Breathy whispers upon her skin.

Savoring memory as your breath takes her in.

Feathery kisses…secrets untold,

as all her passions nearly unfold.

Wishful dreaming…real or pretend?

The core of her being…she let you in.

Receiving your flower…feeling such power.

A wish she made, and it was granted.

Yet…only in her dreaming.

A single hope believed

A single hope believed.

Toss and turn, tears that burn,
my beating heart be still.

Toil and trouble, life a struggle,
too many emotions to feel.

This way, that way, hit the wall.
Tears and laughter, pure disaster, just before the fall.

Cling to this, cling to that.
Nothing touched is real.

Truth a lie, you want to die,
walking death that breathes.

An encouraging word, kindness blind!
Faith, that intercedes.

A single hope believed.

Run & Hide

Choices bare, life not fair.

Silly smiles forced to wear.

Hidden pain, to what gain?

Seeking answers uncovering disaster,

shelter sought from the rain.

Tossing, turning, tortured burning,

endless urgings, insanity merging.

Saving, not thyself.

Rules abide, run and hide!

Time stands still for none.

Wish it away…yet you stay.

Another tortured day, it comes.

Agonized worry, trembling hands –

On shaky ground you now stand.

Close your eyes, a new disguise.

Away you go, deep into dreaming,

to a safe and distant land.

The Wind

Blue black night...
stars burn bright...
Musical whispers in the wind.

Slowly I turn with open arms,
gently, you come in.
Caressing my face,

altering the pace, in
unearthly measure.
I can feel my hair blow in the wind.

You astound me...
peace surrounds me.
I am me, again!

I feel you all around me.
No part you leave untouched.
Natural and free,

my true love and me.
I breathe you in,
my life sustaining power.

For now is the hour,
carrying me away
on the wind!

The Forest

Illustration by Faye Fleming

The Forest

Anxious I was to go out and play,
I'd heard a tale of a fairy that day.
'Mother, I'm off to the forest to play!'

'Aye, you're not! From the forest you'll stay!
It's not safe –it's loaded with bear, for heaven sake!
There's –all kinds of things in there.

Banshee's child! they run wild!
Their mischief might well keep you there.
From the woods, I say... you stay away!'

There it was, pure confirmation.
The forest now, my destination!
Without another moments hesitation,
I was on my way! I had a wish, a fairy myth,
I simply had to go!

I entered the forest –I heard the wind –it
seemed to whisper; 'Please come in!'
My skin it prickled, I got a chill,
but it didn't scare me, I was excited, still.

I walked forever –it was getting late,
I'd never find those bloom'n fairy, at this bloody rate!
When my tummy grumbled, my excitement crumbled,
and it was getting dark! I hadn't seen a single bear, no
banshee's were about. Flopping down upon the ground,
I began to pout.

I leaned against a gigantic tree.
That was when I began to see!
The stars above began to dance,
sending my mind into a magical trance.

*'Those that seek us, surely find us –we
would never leave you, in a state of blindness.'*

Continued On Next Page

I rubbed my eyes with both my fist.
The forest transformed by a twist of her wrist.
I of certain, was overwhelmed!
There, before my very eyes…the Sidhe realm.

Surreal it was, below and above, surrounded now by
fairies of love. I heard a tune, strange to ear,
the most beautiful sound you could hope to hear.
It was beckoning me to follow.

I jumped to my feet, only there to meet –
the Sidhe Queen! With gossamer wings, and sparkly
things, she glowed just like the moon.

She was as fragrant as a garden of flowers,
fresh in bloom. Her voice flowed gently, like that of a
stream, not capable of harshness, much-less a scream!

'Come…partake of our feast!' She beckoned.
There before me, the most delectable banquet I had
ever seen! The fairies encircled me, all began to sing.

There were all sorts of goodies, sweet and sticky things!
It was all so large in proportion, as only such in your
dreams! I ate honeycomb, sipped nectar, drank an odd
sweet brew! The more I seemed to eat! The more I
wanted to!

There were fairies of every shape and size.
They were all different colours too! The only thing they
had in common, were wings, and iridescent eyes!

'Now! They shouted, it's time to fly.'
She watched them there from her spot, as they took to
the sky.

I felt strange, started to change –I could feel my back
as it began to rearrange! I looked to my feet –no shoes,
did my eyes meet. For they, in my delight, Had
disappeared! I stretched my legs, stood tiptoe.

Continued On Next Page

I peeped over my shoulder. I guessed, but didn't know.
'Yes!' I shouted, when I could see.
'Gossamer wings, just for me!'

The queen, she laughed, stepping out of my path,
as I extended my wings to fly. I sang, I danced, upon the
stars and moon I pranced. For now, I was truly free.

We flew over the mountain tops, the oceans fair.
We flew faster than the birds, or any fowl of air.
I waved to the mortals far below, but, I, as a fairy, they
did not know.

Causing a thought to ponder, I had to wonder…
Could it be? In a panic, I flew hard. I flew fast,
It was morning now, night had past. I sat and waited in
mother's garden. But when she entered,
she couldn't see me there!

I shrieked, I flapped and fluttered, I spat, and I sputtered.
She shewed me away like a bug! Mother, it's me, your
daughter, mother, it's me, the one you love! Oh, please
mother…I really need a –hug?

'Your mother no longer sees you…
a fairy you've become. A fairies life is very nice, a dream
that comes, but not without a price.'

I closed my eyes, dropped my head, now feeling rather
numb, from what the fairy said. Oh, what had I done? A
simple wish, a fickle dream, sought after. Now it seemed
my simple dream had turned into pure disaster!

Mother had warned me, but I didn't listen. Now I have
wings that shimmer and glisten. However the fairy had
better think twice, if they think I am willing, to stay tiny as
mice!
I want my mother, and I want her now! I just have to
figure it out. Oh how, how, how?

Continued On Next Page

My tummy growled, then the big oak spoke!
'Careful young one, what you allow the imagination to
invoke!'

I jumped to my feet, nearly three feet, and stared at the
monstrous thing. 'Did you speak to me?' I questioned.
I looked around, not a fae to be found.

The gigantic oak, began to laugh! 'The journey you
embarked has left you well marked.' He smirked.
'The forest is a magical place, all sorts of secrets here.
However, most forget! And for an unbelieving mind, nary
a fairy, nor magic find.'

I turned full circle, looked all around. He was right,
nary a fae in the realm. Had I dreamt it? Had it all been
in my mind? I had to hurry, had to run, for now the sky
was out of sun.

'Supper's in the oven, wash up, then go to bed'!

Her mother was glowing, smiling… knowing.
However, it was all she said.

The End

The Dance

Come...dance with me... he whispers.
She holds her breath, heart beats like thunder.
She hesitates, is it any wonder?
She turns to him knowing what she will see.
If she goes to him now, will she ever be free?
Her mind warns-run...hurry lass, flee!
Her eyes hot with liquid, now drip to the floor.
Why is he here? He doesn't love her anymore.
Unable to speak, her knees feel weak.
What havoc he's played on her heart so bleak.
Glancing around, seeking reprieve,
desolate discomfort, she needs to leave!
All is quiet, still as death.
Finding it impossible still,
to catch her breath.
She closes her eyes,
remembering her dreams,
and promises stolen.
She holds up her head, gives him her hand.
Now she hears it, the distant band.
He pulls her close. She looks into his eyes.
She sees him now, not in disguise.
Foolish no longer, now she's wise.
Around and around –
Twirling, there on the floor.
Her heart whispers gently,
he can't hurt you anymore.
The music ends, no time to pretend.
Smiling wickedly; a shameless grin.
She whispers softly...
Now is the time, the dance is over,
this... the end.

Sweet Dreams, That Carry Me to You

Sweet dreams,
that carry me to you.
Knee high heather, lavender fields.
Warm sun upon my face.

Gently, winds carry me now to
our sacred place.
Our secret garden,
where love was born.

No regrets, nothing forlorn.
Soft kisses upon the skin,
forgetting harshness,
a world of pretend.

Often I'm asked –
Where've you been?
No words are spoken…
I merely grin.

On a warm summers day,
or a quiet whisper of wind.
Against soft falling snow,
in our garden.

Only love,
and tenderness do I know.
My safe haven,
there in the distance.

It's where I go.
Sweet dreams,
that carry me to you.
Our secret garden,

an abundance of love.
Far better is the dreaming imagination.
The weaving of pleasures gestation.
You will find me there often.

Sweet dreams, that carry me to you.

She Cries

With a heavy heart,
and tears in her eyes –She glares out the
window as the rain falls from the skies.
Wanting so badly to expel her disguise –

She cries
Forgetting briefly, from whence she come.
The Images in her mind, always the same.
Ever in her tormented heart,
nothing but pain –

She cries
Was she destined for this?
Was her life never to change?
Feeling as though there should always be more,
was a wee bit of happiness too much to ask for?

She cries
Longing for tomorrow, on a pain, and a sorrow –
Holding to her dreams of the coming morrow,
waking each day, realizing she's alone again.
Looking up to the heavens –a sarcastic grin,
whispering lightly a soft 'amen' –

She cries
Visions of herself, merely going through the motions,
everyday life, without true love, or emotions.
Yesterdays spent, her dreams, simply notions –

She cries
Thinking now, she'd wasted too much time.
It was too late for her to change on a dime.
Her life, her legacy would have to be –

To tell the world –
Don't be like me!
Be who you are, or want to be!
Time is short. Be happy, be free.

Portrait

Born in a place out of time.
A place ahead of the time, that was mine.
Like a portrait with no motion.
Love lost, now merely a notion.

I stand near the mighty sea,
I hear his voice call to me.
Like a portrait with no motion.
The way home lost in the breeze, upon the ocean.

My heart heavy with sorrow, I pray for the morrow –
That my love divine might reach out through
the span of time to find me.
For to what gain is my soul in such a state?

Surely, my life wasn't a mistake!
Like a portrait with no motion.
I long for my true mate.
He holds the key. He knows my name.

For our two hearts, they're the same.
Until he finds me, I shall wait.
Like a portrait with no motion.
Aching with love and undying devotion.

Penance

You've lied in every way.
An innocent of the spirit
shielded your back that was painted
black, and you abused the gift she gave.
Penance she does for kindness shown you.
The price she pays for denial!

She walks through the masses, the muck
of blackness, now only seeking survival.
On her knees she prays –
My God shall lift me up in time,
for I am his, and he is mine.
The only promise now I make –

If you find you feel shame, feel disgrace –
Bow your head, pray for grace.
If your heart is pure,
you'll be delivered –save face.
But nothing here is free.
Surely, you know the truth!

If you turn your back, never to
look back, in need you'll always be.
Tortured curses shall haunt you–
Night sweats, nightmares,
images in your head…shadows lurking,
voices smirking…yet hell you've never seen.

White Witches, Black Witches –
Evils in disguise.
However, hard or simple,
Simply… open your eyes!
Remember to love and never despise –
Don't be foolish, words to the wise.

Oh Sweet Memory

Oh Sweet Memory –
Childhood places, freckled faces –
Days in the sun. Laughs and giggles,
running through high clover, down on the farm.
Oh sweet memory.

The smell of fresh hay, on a glorious day.
Take me away…babbling brooks!
Little bare feet, catching tadpoles,
and crawl-daddy's that pinch!
Oh Sweet Memory

A whiff of Mothers supper in the wind.
Planning tomorrow on a whim!
Another day of play,
as we ran home laughing…all the way!
Oh Sweet Memory.

Grandpa sat at the tables head,
as we bowed our heads to pray.
Oh Grandpa! The greatest gift of all!
Grandpa, indeed, a hero to us all.
Oh Sweet Memory.

The family gathering in the yard at night,
after grandpa milked the cows.
The sky full of stars so bright!
Simply a splendor, a child's delight!
Oh Sweet Memory.

Chasing frogs around like crazy –
Lightening bugs in a jar.
Watching them glow across the room,
with sleepy eyes afar!
Oh Sweet Memory.

Dedicated to my Grandpa!
K.C.George

Oh Ireland –

Has been for as long as I can remember,
the echoes of my ancestors. Oh come yea child,
whispered, magically upon the winds.
Oh hear the bagpipes yonder…listen.
Calling me from my home, oh –Ireland.

Carried upon the winds and sea.
My restless soul hungers for its right of birth.
How can it be, that I have been placed so out of time?
How can my ears hear, and my heart feel,
that which I have not known?

In confusion, sadness and dismay…
I ponder all the possibilities, yet…find no peace!
I walked to the cliff-side today.
Gray stones covered in lovely green velvety moss.
Yet another reminder of my lost home, my birthright.

I could journey forth into the lands of my origin.
'Tis true enough! But what would I find?!
Would I be welcomed, or scorned?
I yearn to feel the cool air caress my skin,
to breathe in the air as I stroll through each glen.

I long to hear the songs of old,
as I hear them now in my head.
Oh come yea Sidhe goddess –
Collect me from this time, or calm these silly notions,
plaguing my ever tortured mind.

Bits and pieces tossed all about,
a puzzle I can't seem to quiet make out!
'Tis a good thing indeed! I was blessed with such
things as I am, and a measure of wit!
I'm tired of this game.

I'm Irish after all…I've a temper as well,
I'm prone to fits! I love you Ireland, home of my blood.
I pray for you nightly, to God above!
Oh Ireland –
Oh Ireland –

In The Darkness of My Dreaming

In the darkness of my dreaming –
In the shadows of my mind.
The never ending light of you,
there for me to find.

Even in my waking hours,
I am ever dreaming.
Your guiding light, forever bright,
and gleaming.

A constant reminder,
of tales untold,
bursting in my heart,
yearning to unfold.

Darkness fell, casting its spell…
but only for a time. As if by magic!
Or destinies call…your gentle voice
lifted me from such a great fall.

Now in the darkness, or behind my great wall –
I see your light flicker, I hear your voice call.
I'm no longer afraid –
No…not at all.

In The Darkness of My Dreaming –
Dedicated to Gerard Butler

Night Bird

Falling asleep to the sound of the night-bird.
Something in my lifetime rarely heard.
As I drifted to sleep on the tune of such splendor –
It was whispering to me, your soul surrender.

This was no ordinary hex! I was confused.
I didn't know what to expect.
I walked into the midst of my early dreaming.
As I followed the wee bird, it's angelic singing.

The stars they sparkled all about my bare feet.
And to my astonishment!
I could not speak.
I wanted to laugh, but cried instead.

Was I dreaming? Was I dead?
Then, all went quiet, all went still –
Even the breeze, I could no longer feel.
She wrapped her wings around me –

I must have cried for hours,
as she lulled my pain away
with her song, and unseen powers.
Just before the dawn, before truly awake.

I could hear the morning bird singing –
I understand the meaning.
I was alive!
I felt like singing.

Dreamer

I Am Your Dreamer

I am your Dreamer...

your passion weaver.

I come to you in your dreaming.

I am the wind whisperer...

Listen... hear my whispers on the wind.

It is I, your Dreamer,

that dances beneath the moonlight,

twinkling bright starlight,

the glistening on your skin.

Feel me as I touch you.

It is I, your Dreamer...

Breathe me in!

Whisper my name, believe!

Close your eyes and behold...

Your Dreamer comes.

My Sister Spirit

I spoke the words and you heard them –
I wrote them, and you followed there path.
My Sister Spirit

Destiny draws us together.
Cast into utter darkness,
for reasons we don't understand.
Wickedness –foreign and abstract to such pure of heart.
Together we are strongest.
We shall best the evil that wronged us!
My Sister Spirit

Never fear…
I hold the power,
'tis only now, I await the hour.
The strength is in the mind…the magic, in believing.
The spell cast, even now un-weaving.
Listen…can you hear it?
My Sister Spirit

Magic words in whisper, evil can't resist her.
Be still, can you feel it?
Broken hearts will heal, don't be afraid to feel.
Languish not, in yesterday, nor moments yet to come.
Live for the moment, it's so much more fun!
My Sister Spirit

Relish in the beauty. Be happy in your skin…
For real beauty glows outward,
comes from within.
The evil that taunts us,
soon shall pass, at last!
My Sister Spirit

Then tables turn, our spirits a haunting burn,
tormenting them relentlessly, forever!
We shall gather the moments that please us best –
Saying with laughter, goodbye to the rest!
My Sister Spirit

My Heart Lies to My Soul

Although I'm fair, just, in truth –
My heart lies to my soul.
It hides its needs, due self, for others.

In vain, it cries, 'save yourself'!'
For you –they shall never discover.
I quiet my thinking, content I be –

When a small child they place upon my knee.
My face it smiles, I've no control.
Yet, my heart bleeds, but they don't know.

What lies ahead for this wee soul? I shudder.
Was one thought given to the many?
I think not! No, not any.

A selfish notion set into motion…
Another now is born.
Trudging through life in search of itself…

battling for better only to discover,
what I now know and shudder.
To do our part would be a start –

My heart lies to my soul.

My Heart Belongs To Me

And there inside all the secrets of life,
and no one knows. I guard and protect it,
my treasures within. My life as it seems,
is anything but dreams.

But never fear my little heart,
for as we are all too familiar –
Imagination calls to me, and I must surrender.
If it were possible, and there must be a way.

In my safe and little world, I would always stay.
Rudely, reality awakens me, and once again, I go.
Return to you, my little heart,
as soon as I am done.

My little world that knows me, and loves me as I am.
Betray myself? I think not! My heart belongs to me.
Imagination, my best friend.
My little world within.

What a shame it truly is, that no one can come in.
For everyone, is not this brave, to live where I do.
But if by chance,
there comes someone –

Who can fathom the unreal?
Only a fleeting thought…my heart, be still.
Imagination, my best friend.
My heart belongs to me.

My Ghostly Lover

My ghostly lover calls to me –
I hear his voice and go.
He calls to me from the distance. I offer no resistance.

He flows through my veins
like an intoxicating wine.
His presence there sublime.

My ghostly lover seduces me, body and mind.
His words are magic.
Working spells on the heart.

To live without them,
would tear me apart!
Leaving me to die of a broken heart.

My ghostly lover hides not his hunger.
It's there in his eyes, it shakes me to my core.
With in mere seconds, reducing me to beg for more.

A master of the art –His erotic song.
Delicately stroking my imagination –
Calming my storm.

My ghostly lover calls to me,
and I must surrender.
My Ghostly Lover –

My Blue Prince

Oh my Blue Prince!
So sleek, and fine you are!
So rare is your character… 'My Blue Prince'.
I wish to live amongst such finery from wince you come.
The kiss of death I'd gladly accept,
if you'd make me your bride.
*

Hello my Dreamer Fairy.
My Blue Prince said to me.
Come take a chance, he whispered –
Take a chance with me!
I will show you the love you're lacking,
for in all love matters, I don't believe in slacking.
And you my precious Dreamer, have been hurt so much
already.
Come my darling, hurry…
I've made plans for us already –Take the leap!
I promise, you won't regret it!
*

Poor Dreamer Fairy…so afraid to feel,
she just couldn't believe her 'Blue Prince',
was really, really, real. Yes, she believed in magic,
for she's a fairy after all. But could she believe such a
handsome prince, with such a tale so tall? She
bargained to the prince. To give her a bit of time!
*

He promised to her then…vowed his very honour!
He would love her forever…from this time to the other.
Vowing he would only be hers, there'd never be another.
His declaration of love, weakening her reserve…
The love he offered, was a love she deserved.
*

I marry you Blue Prince, upon this very day!
Forever in my heart, you shall always stay!
Never, have I known such love.
*

Continued On Next Page

*

Saying their vows, there that day,
Fairy Dreamer rejoiced in delight, truly not knowing her
dreadful plight!
The Blue Prince was an evil sort,
he knew what he had planned.
Now he held her, in the palm of his hand.
*

You're mine now Dreamer!
Kiss your mate! He instructed.
*

Dreamer gladly did his bidding, for she loved
him deeply, she'd not been kidding. His poisonous kiss
would be fatal, none had ever survived.
Only, after the kiss, he felt weak –
Yet Dreamer –she still thrived!
*

Was a foolish thing for you to do! She spat!
Now you get what you deserve!
I'm a Fairy, Dreamer…
Your kiss backfired my love!
You only get what you give,
when you fall in love with a fairy!
The fairy –always survive!

The End

I'm in love with you

What would they do, if they only knew?
I hide in constant fear.
Survive the darkness because of my dream.

Will I ever be brave enough to let go,
to let them know?
I have a dream I need to live out!

I'm in love with you! You know it's true.
Reach to me, the way I reach to you!
Hold me close, don't ever let go!

Help me spread my wings, break free!
Show me how to live, to just be me.
Help me find the will to forsake my every fear.

I see my dreams when I look at you.
Only a love as strong as mine,
deeper than the sands of time.

Have you the power to set me free?
Do you hold the sacred key?
I believe you do!

I can feel it, and I believe you feel it too.
What would they do, if they only knew?
I'm in love with you.

I can't survive without my dream.
I've given all I can, given all I am.
But they can't take my dream.

What would they do, if only they knew?
I hide in constant fear.
Survive the darkness because of my dream.

I'm in love with you.

If I were a breeze

If I were a breeze,
I would be the air you breathe –
A life sustenance refreshing your soul,
sustaining your life.

I would gently wipe your brow when you labor,
If I were a breeze.
I would softly kiss your skin,
while you rest, to insure your comfort.

If I were a breeze,
I would whisper to you
when you are lonely…singing to you the
ancient love songs now forgotten.

If I were a breeze, I would shelter you
when the storms come to haunt you.
For I could wrap myself around you,
and they could see not.

If I were a breeze, so much I would do for you.
But as you know, I'm not.
So for now love, I whisper to the elements.
So hear my song…it comes to you on the winds.

Feel the prickle on your skin,
warm and gentle breeze.
Hear me as I call your name,
as I dance about your head.

There –There –
Impossible as it seems.
Shhh, 'tis me, She grins…
If I were a breeze.

I surrender

Lonely still,

I stare out my window again.

I have to find peace somehow within.

Like a ghost, I wander,

too weary to ponder.

Is not the first time, nor the last –

I know this well from the past!

Will love grow, can it last?

Time passes very fast.

Will I wake in regret, paying

homage to what once was?

I surrender.

No fight left, my spirit beaten –

No prize now for the reaping –

No more tears, no more weeping.

I surrender.

I Believe

I believe you deny what's true.
I believe you love me too.
I'll shout to the world one day,
That I'm in love with you.

I hide my heart now, that's true…
But I can't deny the truth with a lie!
You're in my every thought,
each moment passing by.

My secret hopes set into motion,
my every dream of you,
a forever devotion.
A lifetime of distance.

Yet, our hearts beat as one.
Frivolous resistance…
loves strength persistent.
I believe you deny what's true.

Do try to remember, even into denial,
that if ever you falter, love is the key to survival.
And that! –You shall have always.
Even beyond our passing.

I believe.

I Am Your Lady

I am your lady –
I surrendered my love to you.
I've crossed the surreal of time.
You are truly mine.

Now surrender sir! your love to me.
I heard your voice call out to me,
you drew me through the midst of time.
Now tell me sir…is your love not mine?

I danced the dance of life,
beneath the beaming moon.
I cried into the winds of time,
willing your soul to bind with mine.

And you sir, surrendered.
Surely now you know,
there's no other place for you to go.
I am your lady –you are mine.

You might turn your back for a time,
but you'll call me back, because you're mine.
I surrendered all I am to you. No one else will ever do.
No one can love you like I do –I am your lady.

I am your lady.

Husband

Desired by the many, aye! so fine.
Pleased am I, you are mine.
Moon light dances across your face,
now as you slumber.
I can't help but watch you as you breathe,
in admiring wander.

Aye, in me you stir such need. If I could lock you away,
keep you in greed, I would indeed!
You are perfect in form.
Your skin golden, warm.
Your dark lashes and lovely long hair,
all part of what make you so fine, so fair.

I taste still, your sweet kisses,
your mouth is soft and sweet as bee-pollen.
Heaven help me, I have fallen.
I breathe the scent of you,
in all awareness.
'Tis intoxicating, in all fairness.

I lay naked in your arms, unashamed and bold.
Husband, look at me –
It is your wife, you hold.
You've been all things to me, for so long.
How I wonder,
could things go wrong?

Our love perfect, as a beautiful song.
Thank God...you and I,
are both this strong.
I plan to love you,
till this life is gone.
Husband.

How will you remember me?

Love me now, so I can know.
Don't wait until the time I go.
How will you remember me?

Will you close your eyes and see my face?
Will another soon, take my place,
fill up your void, my empty space?

Will you remember how you made me cry?
The look on my face, when we said goodbye?
How will you remember me?

You've worked so hard for all you gave,
but it's my heart that needed saved.
If you love me any, give up this world, give up the many!

I need no other, no, not any!
Don't kneel above me, declaring your love.
Love me now so I can know.

Don't wait until the time I go.
When you think of me, will you hear my laughter?
Will it bring you joy now, and ever-after?

You're so good, in so many ways.
Yet, I've been alone, far too many days.
Time we could have spent together.

Nights you could have held me till the morrow,
now are gone in bitter sorrow.
I've loved you beyond reason.

Loved you for so many season.
Love is blind, or so they say! And blind you must be.
For how else, can I exist and you not see me?

How will you remember me?

Honour High

But o so low…

I prayed ye not, there to go.

Nay, heed my words…

Hearts beating like drums…

Ah! But for a time,

'twas sweet

and o such fun.

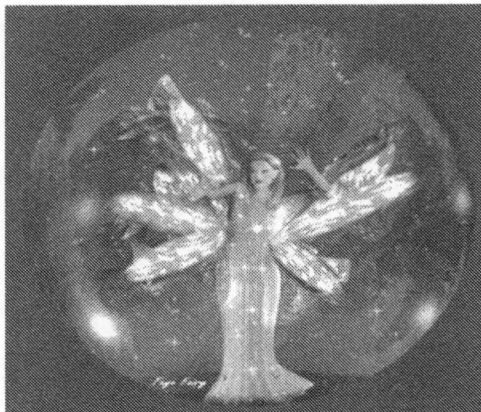

Your Fairy of Love

Born you were...
was destined to be!
A free airy spirit,
happy and free.

Magic in your blood,
you come of age.
Ancient memories,
a roaring flood!

Power denied by
all you know.
Too bizarre!
They can't know.

Into shadows dreaming.
A child of nature has come.
A fairy free!
A star twinkles in her eye.

Flaming hair in the wind does fly.
Lucky you, to gain her love.
She'll guard your life,
engaging all strife.

Your fairy of love.

Evil Haunts

From where does it come, this evil so dark?
The soul cries out, as it try's to embark.
Its taunts relentless, it leaves its mark.
When least expected, it waits in the dark.

It hungers now for even the heart.
Search for peace, trying so hard.
Mind, body, and soul. It knows no bounds.
This dismal evil, it wants it all.

It lurks in the most unsuspected places.
It waits you out, beats you down.
To its gain, for if you fall. Drives you mad.
Loving the most when leaving you sad.

You hold the key, you know you do!
Everything now depends on you.
Battle this dragon. Allow it to flee!
Only then, can your mind be free.

Let it go, leave it behind.
Never again, give it such reign.
You've too much to lose, by it's gain.
The evil that haunts you is the worst of it's kind.

For it's the evil you harbor, deep in your mind.
It waits to ruin you, if you give it the time.
Keeper of this evil deceiver –
Use your power. Use your mind.

Life is a gift, our time on earth swift.
How you view life is up to you.
Take it for granted, take it in strife!
Simply be thankful for such precious life.

Wallow in pity, cry and shame.
Damn the evil, don't play the game.
Acknowledge your strength. Allow evil to flee.
A hero, a victor, you shall see.

You Feel Forced ?

I'm forced to live a life that's yours.
I'm forced to do the thing's you won't.
To entertain the folks you don't.
To accept the fact you love them most!
I'm forced to always hold my tongue,
forced, to care for your other families young!
I'm told I can, I'm told I can't.
Then I'm told, not to rant!

Everyone around... all love you,
but when I'm gone what will you do?
No one left will want to stay...
for to find a bed might prove
a test, not to mention all the rest!
I clean the tubs the toilets too!
In fact, there's nothing, I don't do!

You say you work, isn't that enough?
Well, NO! it's not! Life is tough.
But never fear! Freedom is near...
you can live the life you crave.
But be advised, find a cave!

I can work a nine to five,
tend my bees, and tend my hive.
I can do it all and never strive!
Now I wish you well in all you do,
I pray you find someone else as true,

But most of all...I hope they're just like you!
Just remember when you do,
find a cave dweller, more like you!
Then if they try to force you to bed,
you can merely conk them, in the head!

Now, I'm sorry to rush, don't tell me to hush.
I must be on my way. What was that? No, I can't stay.
What'd you say? Coerced –forced. A donkey, a horse!
Yes, that's right, you feel forced!

What about Me?

You're in a hurry, no! you can't wait.
Oh I can't, I'm gonna be late!
I'm really busy, I don't have the time!
Life's a blast!

But, what about me?

I'm really hungry, hurry up!
What was that? What'd you say…do you
mind? Move out of the way,
I'm watching TV!

But, what about me?

I have to go, my friends await, oh
don't pout, I washed my plate!
I won't be long, I'm doing nothing wrong.
It's getting late, you don't have to wait.

But, what about me?

Seconds, minutes, hours piled high,
days turned to years. Why, Why, Why?
This way, that way, every which way!
Nothing, and everything still the same.

But, what about me?

You wouldn't listen, you wouldn't try!
I think it's time I say goodbye!
Now I'm in a hurry, I can't wait!
Oh don't pout, and please don't cry.

But, what about me?

Render me breathless!

When you look at me,
see my soul.

Then render me breathless
with your words,
allowing me to know.

When you hold me in loves embrace,
touch my face. Taking me from here,
to a magical place.

When you kiss me, leave me breathless.
Leaving no part untouched,
no part of me restless.

With all you are,
render me breathless!

~ She whispers in the wind ~

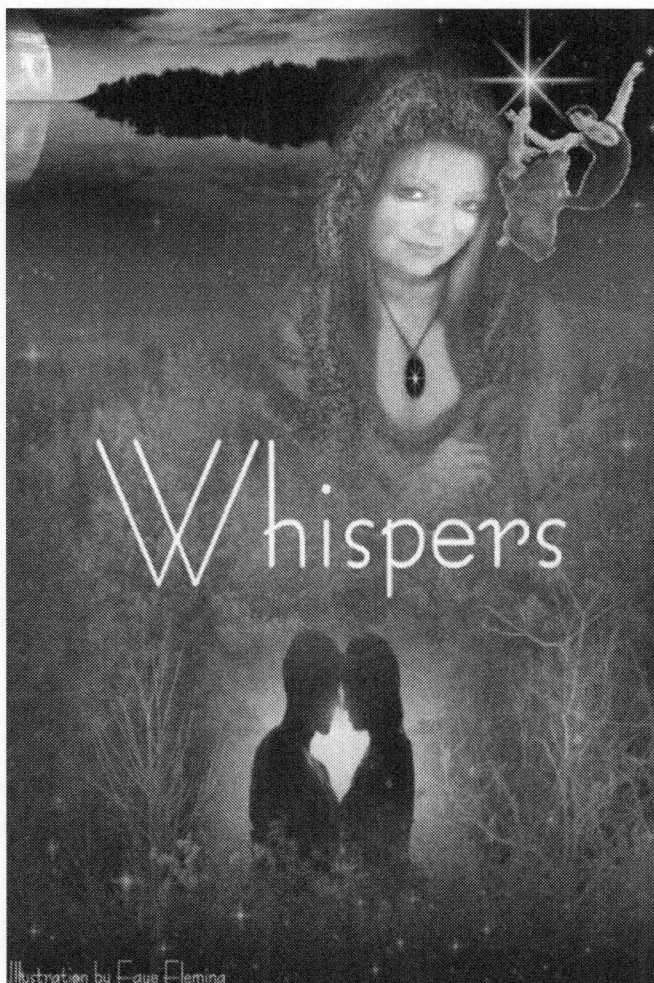

Illustration by Faye Fleming

~ She hears his voice & calls to him ~

Whispers

As I walk amongst the trees and fern,
and watch them as the colours turn.
I think of how the way we are,
I wonder if we'll go this far.

Will we let the changes take the course?
Will you be mine, and I be yours?
Maybe from the winds we'll hide,
bearing our sorrow deep inside.

When I look up to the sky,
I dare the spirits to deny,
a love they said that we would find.
Our sadness we would leave behind.

They tell me things I know are true,
about the love, I share with you.
I feel that they are on our side,
and one day you will be my bride.

So come sweet love and take the chance,
share this life of true romance.
Let the darkness slip away,
I promise you ~'I love you Faye'.

She whispers in the wind.
She hears his voice, and calls to him.
Will you battle all my dragons?
Are you my 'Blue Knight'?

Do I dare let you in? I knew you long ago.
In that, I need not pretend.
Ever, in the shadows of my mind, wherever I go.
Your love always there, for me to find.

Continued On Next Page

~

Only destiny plays her hand,
rendering me helpless, at her command.
I roam in darkness, among the mortal.
I await the time for an open portal.

I will find my way to you in time.
When the time is right,
you shall lead me out of the night.
Casting sorrow and sadness aside.

As we walk together in our plight.
Amongst the fern we shall be.
We shall linger until the darkness
of night, falls upon our heads.

You will lay me down, placing
sweet kisses upon my face, battling all my
dragons, chasing them from that place.
All the tears and pains we've suffered, washed away.

Amongst the fern, beneath the stars of night,
aye, your bride, I shall be that night.
My great victor, we will have won the fight.
I promise you ~I love you, 'My Blue Knight'.

~

~ *Dans l'obscurité, mon amour, j'attends l'heure* ~

Your Memory

My days grow ever longer.
I thought by now, I'd be stronger.

Your memory haunts my very existence.

I thought I knew where you stood.
Somehow, along the way, I must have misunderstood.

Your memory haunts my very existence.

You've said goodbye…I never thought you would.
I can't release you, I thought I could.

Your memory haunts my very existence.

Babe for you, I have no resistance.
You walked away, set me free.
My breaking heart, says that can't be.

Your memory haunts my very existence.

Hearts are broken everyday, you promised you'd
never break mine. Now all I hear is it will heal in time.

Your memory haunts my very existence.

I try to move on, break away.
The pain, it just won't go away.
No matter how far I travel, you're never far away.

Your memory haunts my very existence.

Must my blood flow cold –before I am free?
My body trembles, my heart grows numb.
Yet…
Your memory haunts my very existence.

A Rebel Soul

I fell hard in all pretense.
My heart stands now in full defense.
No sign to find of simple decency.
I walk, I breathe, a living thing.

I've earned my portion of human dignity.
No longer asleep to unrivaled simulation,
fictitious personifications of the humbled and kind.
For however stupid! I'm not blind.

Come what may…bearing human kindness.
The world around us merely reflections.
Each, and every one of us playing a part.
When you look around, what do you see?

Do you see what's there, or what you want to see?
You might not know me!
Or maybe you do!
Yet, I'm unimportant, at least to you.

Nonetheless… who are you?
Steadfast in conviction…
O watchful eye, the waiting beast starves,
to make you cry.

Come! I'm ready…your heart cries out.
I love the world, there's no doubt.
A rebel soul…
A friend I shout!

Away From Home!

Away from home, my love labors every day,

to make me comfortable, in every way.

Away from home, leaving me to weep.

He keeps me in finery, nothing cheap!

Our riches are many, too great to count.

But my loves not home, I'm left without.

I've tried to tell him, he hears me not.

Surely there's a way to make him stop!

My love grows weary, away from home.

My bitter heart, nearly stone.

All I want, is for him to be home!

I grow sick with age, and being alone!

In Shadow

A life sentence in shadow,
a near intolerable incarceration.
Withstood only by a forced
sense of pride and honor,
born and bred in ones head.

A longing hunger consummated
by the coming, whilst in deep sleep.
Consuming you in your dreaming.
Mercilessly loves fire licking at your senses,
making you aware of its presence,
even into your waking hours.

Familiarity, a sense of déjà vu.
You reach to turn the key,
knowing what lies beyond the door.
Rudely the vastness of reality and logic
deprive you of what you know is merely a
motion away. Yet... you are stayed.

Why? Why? Your heart echoes.
Closing your eyes, you hear yourself whisper...
be still, you know it isn't real!
What right have any...to judge the many?
What factor determines what one feels?
Who determines, what is false or real?

Which fear, feared the most?
To find your dream a wishful host,
or a love you denied and lost?
Fearing the unknown, facts unproved,
a life sentence in shadow,
a near intolerable incarceration.

In Shadow.

Illustration by Faye Fleming

Awakened By the Winds

Awakened by the winds
soft caress upon my face.
Showered with the sweet fragrance
of Honeysuckle, Lavender and
Magnolia's in full bloom.
Even before my eyes were open,
I knew the day could hold no gloom.
Natures melody, beckoning me to the garden below.
Come, oh come! Born they are, our young!
The fairies sang.
Light as a feather, barefoot and free,
I flew to the garden to see!
Golden flecks flitted from here to there.
New fairy life was everywhere!
Sing us a song mother,
a lullaby please…
Weave a spell bidding us well –
Oh mother will you, please?
Come nigh, she whispered.
Lady bugs, nor beetles,
scraggly weeds or thistle,
weaving spiders, or any spinners,
slugs, nor snails.
Any uncomely thing, nor wagging tails.
No spell, no charm can do you harm, she sang.
For hence! The fairy queen is nigh.
The winds then played a magical tune.
Everything in the garden surreal.
Opening my mind, a new awakening.
Familiar fairy, forever –friends.
Awakened by the winds.

Awakened from my slumber,
I heard your voice and came.
I wrapped myself around you, whispered your name.
Our spirits, bound forever, our hearts, they're the same!
I shall always love you –think of me fondly,
whenever you whisper my name.

MINE

Mine

Close your eyes and hear the calm.
Nothing between us could ever be wrong.
When you're at your weakest, I am strong.
Feel the air upon your skin,
always remember its there I've been.

My whispers soft, caresses gentle.
Dreamy desire runs hot then cold.
I am shy and you are bold.
Only the wise and ancients hold
the secrets that set us free.

Warm words and laughter,
Contentment chased after.
Running from heartache, pain and disaster.
Pieces of puzzles gently placed.
I saw happiness in your eyes, and upon your face.

Smiles sweet as nectar,
careful is love to never reject her.
Spiritual bonding, none to compare.
The peace you felt, there in your chair.
To sever this bond could never be right.

Don't give up now…stand up and fight! You fight the
notions running through your head.
You've tossed and turned alone there in your bed.
You try replacing me with flesh instead, only to find
emptiness in my stead.

Burning desire in all of its greed,
blinds you now of what you need.
Caution now thrown into the wind. Hopeful wishing
comes to an end. You've heard my voice…breathed me
in. It was real…not pretend.

Starving for attention, starving for love, fighting the evil,
the ages of time. I fought for you without reason or
rhyme. Reaching out to you through the sands of time,
to hear you simply say…
You're Mine!

Emotions Stage

The seasons changing yet again,
reminding me yet of him.
Tiny buds begin to bloom.
Red bud trees flower crimson.

Dogwoods pink, white and red with flowers,
images of his eyes, his face, his powers.
The sky so grand and blue,
clouds anew of fluffy cotton.

Life long dreams not forgotten.
The wind breezes past my ear.
Whispering —never fear.
Loves promise on the wind.

Pure hearts love, never ends.
Ages pass —I grow impatient.
Winters past —frozen stages.
Falling snow —the still of dawn.

I cry out loud to not be wrong.
Sudden shudders, prickly fear.
His voice is lost, yet so near.
Lonely pain, deep regret.

Voices of old in heavy sigh,
remember child, you can not die.
Your time will come, steadfast in calm —
The wind a gift, a healing balm.

Your robe is white, your shield is love.
Your words hold magic, use them wise.
The fox he comes in lamb's disguise,
only from you, he does not hide.

Reverse the role, turn the tide!
Remember yourself,
be strong, take pride.
Weather changes, seasons pass.

Continued On Next Page

His love for you will always last.
He knows your name, he hears your voice.
Whisper Dreamer, it's simply a choice.
Calmness comes before the storm.

Wicked comes in every form.
Hear the laughter in your heart.
The blackness comes to smote it out.
Rain of tears, replenished soul.

Peaceful rest you shall know.
The birds will chirp in seasons come.
Standing still, or at a run.
Magic words of riddle, words of rhyme.

His love is true just give it time.
Question not, the unseen mystery –
Await the ghostly hour. In truth,
none yet know how great the power.

Rushing fate could turn it sour.
Treasure that, in which you see,
remember the truth shall set you free!
Seize the moment, the memory yours.

The door shall open…step inside –
When the time is right…you will not hide.
Embrace the love that's already yours.
It will be returned an hundred scores.

Gifts such as these come not from greed –
The gift of love the greatest indeed.
To be given it freely is all you need.
The storm has stilled, your heart be filled.

Emotion's stages, fill the pages.
The moon is full the stars are bright.
A passage of time –another night.
Emotions Stage.

Eyes

Eyes…dark pools.
Sky blues –
Mystic grays, and green.
Ambers light –
Stars of night –
Windows of the soul.
Chanted spell, burning
now your eyes, then
your soul.

Faye Fleming, Author of Paranormal Romance Novel, 'Forbidden' has recently ventured into several genres. She has just finished a children's novel that she hopes to release sometime this year. She is currently working on a sassy romance about the cyber world. And has now compiled this issue of poetry that she has been working on for the last few years. She and her husband now reside on a secluded property overlooking the Floyds Fork in Kentucky. She lives a simple life with her husband of thirty years, along with their two toy poodles. Faye is passionate about most all of the arts. Aside from writing; she loves to dabble in photography, design and illustrations. She and her husband enjoy attending local plays, and musicals. Faye's favourite being 'The Phantom of the Opera' and 'Cats'. Faye's Irish heritage loans to her love of anything Celtic. She says it must be in her blood. She recently became a die-hard fan of Celtic Woman, after attending one of their concerts at Louisville Palace. Faye hasn't decided if she wants to settle into one genre or continue exploring. Her imagination is larger than life. She believes our imaginations and ability to dream are what carry us through life. In addition, says that she has never been bored a day in her life!

From The Heavens,

I Shall Cast Mine Eyes Upon An Earthly Dream

And Shall Smile, For I Was Blessed

Also by Faye Fleming
"Forbidden*" A Paranormal Romance*

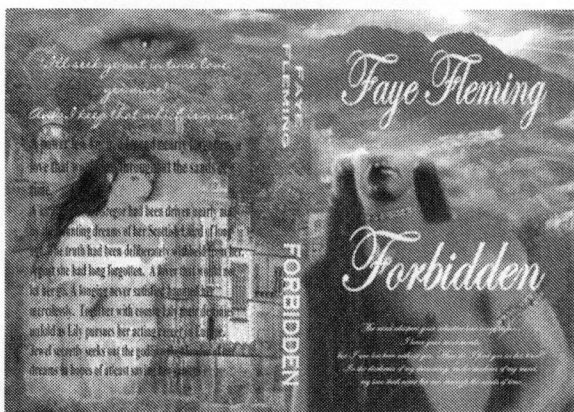

A Power few new, a legend nearly forgotten. A love that would last throughout the sands of time.

Akira Jewel MacGregor had been driven nearly mad by the haunting dreams of her Scottish laird of long ago. The truth had been deliberatly withheld from her. A past she had long forgotten. A love that would not let her go. A longing never satisified haunted her mercilessly.

"I'll seek ye out in time love, yer mine!"

~~~
"Among the Fairies"

A children's novel